Country File
Pakistan

Ian Graham

A+

Smart Apple Media

First published in 2003 by Franklin Watts
96 Leonard Street, London EC2A 4XD, UK

Franklin Watts Australia
45–51 Huntley Street, Alexandria, NSW 2015

Country File: Pakistan produced for Franklin Watts by
Bender Richardson White, PO Box 266, Uxbridge, UK.

Editor: Lionel Bender, *Designer and Page Make-up:* Ben
White, *Picture Researcher:* Cathy Stastny, *Cover Make-up:*
Mike Pilley, Radius, *Production:* Kim Richardson, *Graphics
and Maps:* Stefan Chabluk
Copyright © 2003 Bender Richardson White

Consultant: Dr. Terry Jennings, a former geography teacher
and university lecturer. He is now a full-time writer of
children's geography and science books.

Published in the United States by Smart Apple Media
1980 Lookout Drive, North Mankato, Minnesota 56003

Library of Congress Cataloging-in-Publication Data

Graham, Ian, 1953– Pakistan / by Ian Graham.
p. cm. — (Country files) Includes index.
Contents: Welcome to Pakistan — The land — The people —
Urban and rural life — Farming and fishing — Resources and
industry — Transport — Education — Sport and
leisure — Daily life and religion — Arts and media —
Government — Place in the world.
ISBN 1-58340-239-X   1. Pakistan—Juvenile literature.
[1. Pakistan.] I. Title. II. Series.
DS376.9.G73 2003   954.91—dc21   2003042359

9 8 7 6 5 4 3 2 1

Picture Credits

Pages 1: Eye Ubiquitous/Jason Burke. 3: Eye
Ubiquitous/Peter Barker. 4: James Davis Travel
Photography. 7: James Davis Travel Photography. 8: Eye
Ubiquitous/David Cumming. 9: Eye Ubiquitous/Dean
Bennett. 10: Eye Ubiquitous/Julia Waterlow. 11: Eye
Ubiquitous/Peter Barker. 13: James Davis Travel
Photography. 14: James Davis Travel Photography. 15:
Eye Ubiquitous/Jason Burke. 16: Eye Ubiquitous/Jason
Burke. 17: Eye Ubiquitous/David Cumming. 19 top: Eye
Ubiquitous/David Cumming. 19 bottom: Eye
Ubiquitous/Jason Burke. 20: Eye Ubiquitous/Jason Burke.
21: Eye Ubiquitous/David Cumming. 22 top: Eye
Ubiquitous/David Cumming. 22 bottom: Eye
Ubiquitous/David Cumming. 24: Corbis Images/Charles
and Josette Lenars. 25: Corbis Images. 26: Corbis Images.
27: James Davis Travel Photography. 28–29: Corbis
Images/Jeffrey L. Rotman. 30: Eye Ubiquitous/Jason
Burke. 31: Eye Ubiquitous/Julia Waterlow.

Cover Photo: Eye Ubiquitous/D. Cumming.

The Author

Ian Graham is a full-time writer and
editor of nonfiction books. He has
written more than 100 books for
young readers.

Contents

Welcome to Pakistan

The Islamic Republic of Pakistan occupies the northwest corner of the Indian subcontinent. Pakistan came into being on August 14, 1947, when British rule in India ended. It was created as a homeland for India's Muslims. Its name comes from two Urdu words—*pak* (pure) and *stan* (land).

Pakistan originally consisted of two parts, one on each side of northern India. East and West Pakistan were separated by 995 miles (1,600 km). Then, in 1971, East Pakistan declared independence as Bangladesh, leaving West Pakistan as the country we know today as Pakistan.

Its people are as diverse as its terrain, with their own distinctive languages, dialects, and customs. These have developed during a history lasting more than 10,000 years.

Vehicles on hairpin bends through the Khyber Pass, which links northwest Pakistan with Afghanistan. ▼

The Land

Animals

Mammals:
Markhor (a goat, the national animal of Pakistan), Marcopolo sheep, Sindh wild goat, Himalayan ibex, musk deer, hog deer, black buck antelope, Eurasian brown bear, Asiatic black bear, common leopard, snow leopard, Asiatic cheetah, Eurasian lynx, gray wolf, golden jackal, striped hyena, Indian wild boar, red fox, Bengal fox, rhesus macaque, hanuman langur, and porcupine.

Birds:
Partridge, warblers, shikra, blue rock pigeon, rock nuthatch, red–gilled chough, golden eagle, black eagle, Imperial eagle, black kite, Indian sparrowhawk, Saker falcon, kestrel, hobby, merlin, goshawk, Siberian crane, Eurasian crane, Indian peafowl, Egyptian vulture, and bearded vulture.

Reptiles and Amphibians:
Monitor lizard, marsh crocodile, leopard gecko, Afghan tortoise, Indian python, Indian cobra, horned viper, green turtle, ant frog, tiger frog, cricket frog, burrowing frog, and toads.

Pakistan is a land of extremes—from dry, dusty deserts in the southeast to fertile plains in the eastern and south-central regions, and some of the highest mountains in the world.

Pakistan is divided in two by the Indus River, which starts in Tibet in China and flows across the Himalayas mountain range into the north of the country. The Indus is joined by other rivers flowing from India, and it empties into the Arabian Sea in the south.

To the west of the Indus lie the Baluchistan Highlands. To the east lies the flat expanse of the Indus Plain. The Thar Desert straddles the eastern border with India. In the south, the coastal plain skirts the Arabian Sea. The Kharan Basin lies to the west of the Baluchistan Highlands. The Toba Kakar, Siahan, Kirthar, and Sulaiman mountain ranges all pass through the Baluchistan Highlands.

The northeast of the country is crossed by the towering Karakoram mountain range, with the second-highest mountain in the world after Everest—K2 (also known as Mount Godwin Austen), at 28,251 feet (8,611 m)—and some of the biggest glaciers outside the polar regions.

Profile of the annual rainfall for Karachi on the coast of Pakistan. ▼

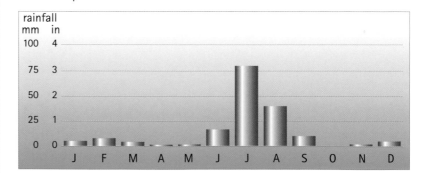

Growing mountains

Pakistan is so mountainous because the part of the Earth's crust on which it sits is pushing its way into the rest of Asia. In fact, the whole Indian subcontinent has traveled about 1,200 miles (2,000 km) into Asia. The enormous forces between these colliding land masses have pushed the ground between them upwards, creating their vast mountain ranges. The process continues today, causing frequent earthquakes in the region.

Climate

Pakistan has extreme variations in temperature and rainfall during the year and from place to place. There are three distinct seasons—the cool season (October to February), the hot season (March to June), and the wet season (June to October). During the wet season, the eastern and central plains receive abundant rain, but there is little rainfall in the arid southern and southeastern desert regions.

Small villages and cultivation terraces cover the foothills of the Karakoram mountain range in northern Pakistan.

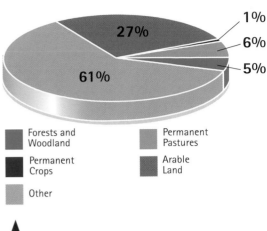

27%

1%

6%

5%

61%

■ Forests and Woodland
■ Permanent Crops
■ Other
■ Permanent Pastures
■ Arable Land

▲
▲ Land use in Pakistan. More than half the land is mountain and desert (defined as "other").

Plants

Pakistan's trees include: Spruce, evergreen oak, cheer pine, deodar (a type of cedar tree), alpine flora, pistachio, juniper, wild olive, wild ash, wild almond, fig, barbery, wild cherry, and makhi.

The People

Many of the peoples who settled in the Indian subcontinent over the centuries have handed down their distinctive cultures and customs through the generations to modern Pakistan. There is therefore no single, or typical, Pakistani culture.

Today, most of the people of Pakistan can be divided into five main ethnic groups—Punjabis, Sindhis, Pathans (Pashtuns), Balochs, and Muhajirs. The Muhajirs are Muslim immigrants who moved to Pakistan from India after independence, and their descendants. Punjabis are the most numerous group, followed by Sindhis.

Pakistanis, such as these fishermen in Karachi, are a mix of Indian, Chinese, east Asian, and Arab peoples. ▼

Language

The official language of Pakistan is Urdu, but less than a tenth of the population speak it as their first language. About half of the population speak Punjabi, which is widely spoken in neighboring northern India. English is also widely spoken in government, the military forces, and higher education.

Population and cultural changes

Pakistan's population has grown rapidly since the country's birth. By 1990, the population was more than three times its size in 1947. It continues to grow at the rate of about two percent, adding nearly three million more people every year.

Pakistan society is patriarchal (male dominated). In most of the country, women have a lower status than men. Wealthier rural families and some urban families observe a practice called *purdah*, in which women of all ages are hidden from view. They live screened off from visitors, and they must cover themselves with concealing clothing when they go outside.

Purdah is in decline, however. The poorest families do not observe it because their women have to work. In the cities, too, fewer families observe it as more young women enter the workforce as independent, educated citizens.

 Children dress in traditional clothes similar to those of adults.

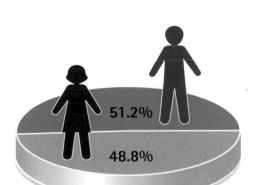

51.2%

48.8%

 There are more men than women in Pakistan's population.

DATABASE

Ancient history

Stone Age people lived near modern Rawalpindi 50,000 years ago. By about 8500 B.C., people were farming crops in Baluchistan. Human settlements spread along the Indus River. By about 2600 B.C., they had developed into the Indus Valley civilization. This flourished until its sudden end in about 1750 B.C., perhaps because of a change in the climate.

🌐 Web Search ►►

► http://www.statpak.gov.pk
General facts and figures from the government of Pakistan's Statistics Division.

► http://www.cia.gov/cia/publications/factbook/geos/pk.html
The Pakistan entry in the CIA World Factbook, with information about the country and its people.

► http://unstats.un.org/unsd/demographic/social/population.htm
Population data provided by the United Nations Statistics Division.

Urban and Rural Life

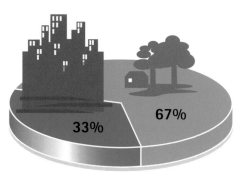

Percentage of Population Living in Urban Areas

Percentage of Population Living in Rural Areas

 Two-thirds of Pakistan's population live in rural areas.

A goatherder tends his flock on hills around his village in the Karakoram Mountains. ▶▶

The Islamic Calendar

The passage of time in Pakistan's towns and villages is ruled by the Islamic calendar. Its starting point is the flight of the prophet Muhammad from Makkah (Mecca) to Medina, in Saudi Arabia, in 622 A.D. The Islamic calendar is lunar (based on the movements of the moon). A year has 354 or 355 days, and the 12 months are 29 or 30 days long.

The majority of Pakistan's population lives in the country's extensive rural areas. Living standards vary enormously between rural villages and major cities.

Pakistani families are especially close. It is common for two or three generations to live together. Wealthier urban families live in modern apartments or large houses. The less well-off may have only one or two rooms in which to house parents, children, grandparents, uncles, and aunts. Homes and workplaces in cities are built from concrete or brick and have their own water supply and sewage system.

Most of Pakistan's cities have grown and developed naturally over centuries, but its capital city, Islamabad, is a modern planned city with streets laid out in a grid pattern. The city is divided into different zones for government, commerce, industry, residence, and recreation.

Village life

Living conditions in rural villages are more difficult than those in the cities. Houses are often made from bricks held in place by mud or clay. The roof may be made from corrugated iron weighted down with rocks, or from branches and leaves. Rural houses often have no running water or sewage system, but there may be access to a shared clean-water supply such as a well or standpipe.

Home produce

Most rural families produce at least some of their own food. It is common to keep a goat or two for milk, and perhaps a buffalo to pull a plow. The milk is used to make cheese, butter, and yogurt. A variety of vegetables, beans, and peas are grown. Meat may be in such short supply that it is eaten only on ceremonial occasions. Flour products, such as *naan* and *chapatis* (types of bread) are the dietary staples, washed down with *chai* (tea) or *lassi* (milk with the curds and butterfat removed).

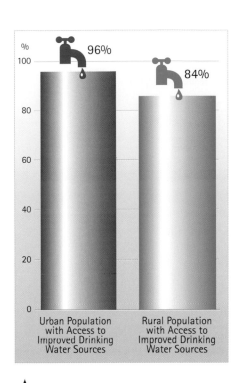

Percentage of urban and rural populations with access to sources of clean drinking water.

◄◄ A busy crossroads in Karachi. In the city center, there are apartment and office buildings but no tall skyscrapers.

Web Search ►►

► http://unstats.un.org/ unsd/demographic/ social/hum–set.htm
Urban and rural population statistics for many countries, including Pakistan.

11

Farming and Fishing

Farming and fishing

Production in tons (tonnes):

Sugar cane	60,860,000 (55,200,000)
Wheat	19,956,000 (18,100,000)
Rice	5,126,800 (4,650,000)
Cotton	1,949,300 (1,768,000)

Fishing catch 680,000 (616,500)

Agriculture is the most important part of Pakistan's economy. It employs about half of the country's workforce and makes up a quarter of its gross domestic product (GDP).

Wheat is the staple food and the most widely grown crop. Sugar cane, cotton, and rice are grown mainly as cash crops. Cotton earns valuable export income and also supplies the domestic textile industry. Rice is grown mainly on the Indus River plain, where the soil is enriched by sediments washed down from the mountains.

One crop that has attracted worldwide attention is opium. A large proportion of the world's heroin—a harmful illegal drug—comes from opium poppies grown along the Pakistan-Afghanistan border. The government has been reducing this problem by giving farmers seed for other crops and providing alternative work for people.

Farming Regions

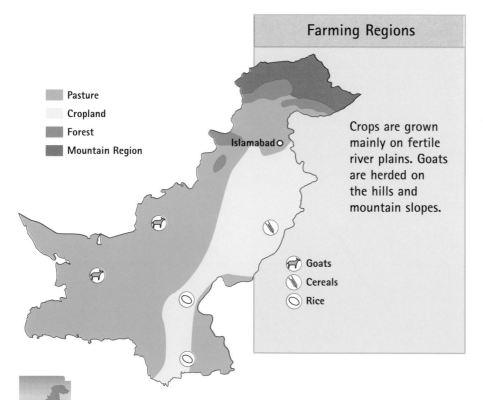

Pasture
Cropland
Forest
Mountain Region

Islamabad

Crops are grown mainly on fertile river plains. Goats are herded on the hills and mountain slopes.

Goats
Cereals
Rice

Seasons and livestock

There are two main seasons for agriculture: *kharif* begins between April and June and ends between October and December; *rabi* begins in November or December and ends in April or May. The main winter crops are wheat, cumin, and barley. In summer, onions, potatoes, and several other vegetables are grown. Livestock farming produces milk, beef, mutton, poultry, and wool.

Irrigation

In Pakistan's driest areas, large numbers of water pumps have been installed to bring more water to the surface for agriculture. Pakistan now has one of the world's biggest irrigation systems, built along the Indus and adjoining rivers with money from the World Bank and the U.S. government. This has enabled the country to become self-sufficient in food grains. Unfortunately, each time the wet soil dries in the sun, a layer of salt forms on the surface, eventually making the soil infertile.

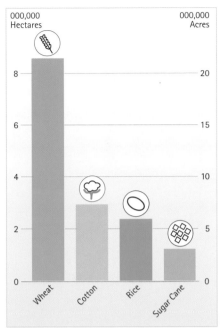

000,000 Hectares
000,000 Acres

▲ Area under cultivation in Pakistan for major crops. Wheat is by far the most widely grown crop.

A farmyard near Lahore. Most farmers still use animal power and simple machinery to cultivate the land. ▼

Fishing

Most Pakistanis eat very little fish. The average consumption is only 4.4 pounds (2 kg) per year—about one-third of the amount eaten in Britain or the U.S. The fishing catch includes sardines, anchovies, and sharks. Shrimp, which makes up a tenth of the catch, is highly prized because of its export value.

Web Search ►►

► http://www.statpak.gov.pk/crops.htm
Information about Pakistan's crops from the government's Statistics Division.

13

Resources and Industry

Mining and industry

	Thousand tons (tonnes)
Cement	10,500 (9,500)
Coal	3,435 (3,116)
Pig iron	1,650 (1,500)
Crude steel	550 (510)
Gypsum	415 (377)
Soda ash	250 (230)
Caustic soda	240 (220)

Natural gas
31 billion cubic yards
(24 billion cubic m)

Crude petroleum
20 million barrels
(1 barrel = 42 gal (159 L))

Agriculture is so important to the Pakistan economy that the land itself is a valuable resource. Most of the country's natural resources are in the form of minerals extracted by mining or drilling.

In all, more than 20 different types of minerals have been found in commercial quantities. These include iron ore, salt, chromite, manganese, sulphur, and copper. Iron ore is mined in large quantities, but it is mostly poor quality. Coal is mined, too, but most of it is also poor quality. Large reserves of limestone are mined to supply the cement-making industry. Oil, first discovered in 1915, contributes to Pakistan's energy needs. Extensive natural gas fields were discovered in the 1950s.

Pakistan's most important industry is cotton textile production. Other industrial products include steel, machinery, paper, chemicals, sugar, vegetable oil, food processing, and fertilizer. Chemical production includes soda ash, caustic soda, and sulphuric acid.

◄◄ Many wooden and metal products are still handcrafted.

Energy

Pakistan's energy needs are rising rapidly as more people use more electrical goods. Energy consumption has tripled since the 1980s. More than half of the country's electricity is generated by power stations that burn oil, gas, or coal. Most of the rest is hydroelectricity, generated by water-powered turbines.

Clothing and footwear

One of the fastest-growing manufacturing industries in Pakistan is the production of leather clothing, footwear, and sports equipment. It is a very labor-intensive business employing more than 200,000 people. Other manufactured goods include pharmaceuticals, aircraft, machine tools, carpets, textiles, and electrical goods such as light bulbs, televisions, radios, and refrigerators.

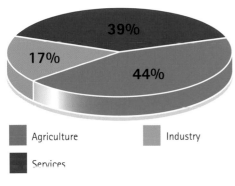

Agriculture

Industry

Services

39%

17%

44%

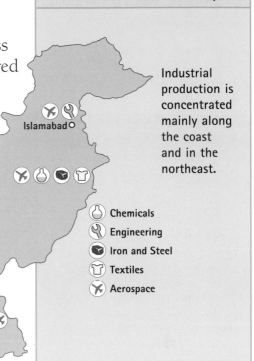

Resources and Industry

Industrial production is concentrated mainly along the coast and in the northeast.

Islamabad

- Chemicals
- Engineering
- Iron and Steel
- Textiles
- Aerospace

Nearly half of Pakistan's workforce is employed in agriculture. "Services" include banking and insurance.

Teenage workers stitch together leather panels to make soccer balls for export.
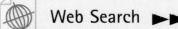

Web Search ►►

► http://www.mpnr.gov.pk/pmdc.html

Web site of the Pakistan Mineral Development Corporation, established in 1974 to explore, plan, develop, and operate mining ventures in Pakistan.

► http://minerals.usgs.gov/minerals/pubs/country/2000/9301000.pdf

A downloadable report on Pakistan's mineral output from the U.S. Geological Survey.

Transportation

Mountain Passes

Travel between Pakistan and its neighbors to the north and west depends on natural passages through the high mountains. There are 200 such passes between Pakistan and Afghanistan alone. The most famous and important is the Khyber Pass, a 32-mile (53 km) long passage through the Hindu Kush. It has been used by invading armies and camel trains for more than 2,000 years. Today it carries a modern highway, a railway line, and an ancient caravan route.

Pakistan is covered by an extensive network of roads, railways, and air routes. Public transportation within towns is mainly by buses, taxis, auto-rickshaws, and *tongas* (horse-drawn carriages). Larger buses, many of them air-conditioned, travel the highways between the major cities.

Pakistan's cities are connected by modern paved highways. The GT (Grand Trunk) Road links Lahore and Peshawar. The Super Highway and National Highway run from Karachi to the interior of Sindh and Punjab. The Indus Highway runs between Peshawar and the southern Punjab. One of the most famous Asian roads, the Karakoram Highway, runs all the way from Islamabad to Kashgar in China. The RCD (Regional Cooperation for Development) Highway links Karachi with Quetta and Taftan on the Iran border.

Railway network

Pakistan's national railway service carries 65 million passengers every year. It operates 228 mail, express, and passenger trains daily. Since the 1990s, its diesel-electric locomotives have been built at a new factory near Peshawar, set up with help from Japan. It still runs much older steam trains in some places, especially for tourists.

◀◀ Buses on a major road in northern Pakistan. Luggage is carried in roof racks.

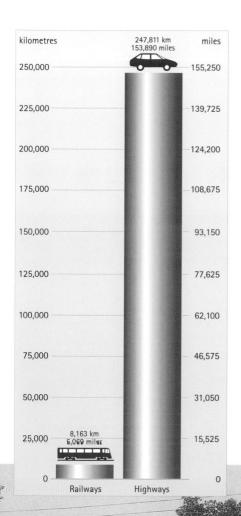

kilometres | miles

247,811 km
153,890 miles

250,000 — 155,250

225,000 — 139,725

200,000 — 124,200

175,000 — 108,675

150,000 — 93,150

125,000 — 77,625

100,000 — 62,100

75,000 — 46,575

50,000 — 31,050

8,163 km
5,069 miles

25,000 — 15,525

0 — 0

Railways | Highways

◄◄ Comparison of the length of Pakistan's road and rail networks. Most road vehicles are lorries, trucks, taxis and buses rather than private cars.

Transport

ⓧ Major Airport

— Main Roads

— Railways

Peshawar
Islamabad
Rawalpindi
Gujranwala
Lahore
Faisalabad
Quetta
Multan
Sukkur
Karachi
Hyderabad

Most people travel between cities by road and rail – few Pakistanis can afford to travel by air. The major airports deal with both international and national flights. There are direct flights to Islamabad airport from most parts of Asia.

◄◄ In Lahore, people crowd on to small buses or hire motorized rickshaws or horse-drawn buggies to get around the city.

🌐 Web Search ►►

► http://pakrail.com
Website of Pakistan's national railway service, Pakistan Railways.

► http://www.piac.com. pk/piaspakistan.htm
Information on tourist destinations in Pakistan

► http://www.tourism. gov.pk/road.html
Details of Pakistan's road network.

Education

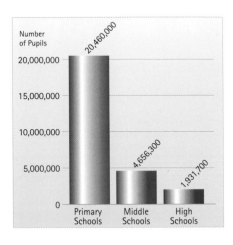

Number of Pupils

20,460,000

4,656,300

1,931,700

Primary Schools | Middle Schools | High Schools

▲ Primary education is free, but many children are unable to attend school.

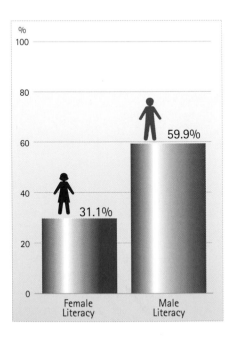

%
100

80

59.9%

60

40

31.1%

20

0

Female Literacy | Male Literacy

▲ Male literacy is low, but female literacy is even lower.

Education in Pakistan is based on the system introduced during the period of British rule. The subjects taught are also similar to those taught in British schools—including math, science, and literature. In addition, there are classes in Urdu (the national language), English, and Islamic studies.

Children enter primary school at the age of 5 and leave when they are 10 years old. They attend middle school for the next three years, until the age of 13. After that, secondary school (high school) lasts for another two years. Then, at the age of 15, they can go on to a technical secondary school or a higher secondary school for two years. For those who have the ability to go further, higher education is provided by universities and colleges.

Literacy and child workers

Despite having such a well-developed education system, the majority of the population is illiterate. The situation is worst in rural areas, where poverty prevents many children from attending school. Instead, they have to help to support their families by working in the fields, looking after the home, or making things to sell.

Female literacy is particularly low. This is because less than one-fifth of girls finish primary school. To make matters worse, not all schools accept girls. Only about one in four primary schools and one in three secondary schools accept girls. Some religious, political, and other organizations are trying to help by setting up informal schools for girls in their own villages. The teachers are chosen from the local community, and villagers have a say in what is taught. These informal schools can be set up in places where there are no state schools, because they cost less than two percent of the cost of a state school.

A schoolboy practices writing Urdu using chalk and a slate.

 An outdoor class at a school in north Pakistan. All the pupils are boys.

Web Search ►►

► http://www.statpak.
gov.pk/social_indicators.
htm

Facts and figures on social issues, including education, from the government of Pakistan's Statistical Division.

► http://unstats.un.org/
unsd/demographic/
social/default.htm

Literacy figures for many countries, including Pakistan, from the United Nations Statistical Division.

Sport and Leisure

Pakistan is a sporting nation. From the smallest village to the biggest cities, Pakistanis play games and follow the fortunes of their favourite teams with great enthusiasm.

Pakistan's national sport is hockey. The national team has won four world championships and gold medals at the Olympic and Asian Games. Jahangir and Jansher Khan dominated squash in the 1980s and 1990s by winning 14 consecutive world championships. Pakistan's boxers, wrestlers and weightlifters have also won international honours. In 1995, Pakistan achieved the remarkable record of holding world championships in cricket, field hockey, squash and snooker at the same time.

Polo started as a sport in Pakistan and neighbouring countries. ▼

Kabaddi

In addition to such team sports as cricket and hockey, a game called *kabaddi* is also popular. It is played by two teams who each try to capture players from the other team. It is thought the game developed in Pakistan about 4,000 years ago as a way of training people in hand-to-hand fighting.

Children play volleyball on a makeshift court in north-east Pakistan. ▶▶

Cricket

Throughout the country, cricket is the most popular game. Successful players, such as Imran Khan and Waseem Akram, have become world-famous. A form of cricket called tape-ball cricket is very popular. Tennis balls are more readily available than cricket balls, but they are too light for cricket. To make them behave more like cricket balls, they have lots of sticky tape wrapped around them.

Music

Until the 1980s, most of the music played and broadcast on TV and radio in Pakistan was traditional folk music. *Qawwali*, a form of music that comes from the Islamic religious tradition, is very popular. In recent years, Western rock music has grown in popularity, especially in the cities and among wealthier people. The most famous of Pakistan's music groups at home and abroad is Junoon. Their style is a blend of traditional and rock music.

Web Search ▶▶

▶ http://www.sports.gov.pk
The sports page of the Pakistan government website giving details of Pakistan's involvement in sports at national and international level.

▶ http://wwwcricinfo.com
A cricket website with a section on the Pakistan team, its players and news of their matches.

Muslim worshippers praying at a mosque.

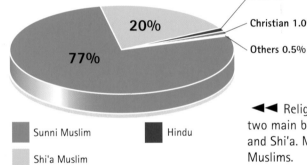

1.5%

20%

Christian 1.0%

77%

Others 0.5%

Sunni Muslim
Shi'a Muslim
Hindu

◄◄ Religion in Pakistan. There are two main branches of Islam: Sunni and Shi'a. Most Pakistanis are Sunni Muslims.

The Hajj

The Koran requires every Muslim to visit the holy city of Mecca, in Saudi Arabia, at least once. Mecca is the birthplace of the prophet Muhammad, the founder of Islam. During the annual pilgrimage to Mecca, called the Hajj, pilgrims perform a series of rites. Each year, many Pakistanis—often only adult males but sometimes whole families—make the journey to Mecca.

Most people shop for food in local street markets like this one in Quetta. ▼

Daily Life and Religion

Daily life in Pakistan is dominated by the traditions of the Muslim faith and the teachings of its holy book, the Koran.

Daily life for a primary school child living on a rural farm begins at about 6:00 A.M. with washing and prayers. Then it is time for breakfast and a walk to school. After returning home in the afternoon, homework and household chores have to be done. Only then is there time for playing with friends before more prayers and then dinner. By 9:00 P.M. it is time for bed. On the weekend, when there is no school, work has to be done in the fields.

The diet in Pakistan consists of four main ingredients—*roti* (bread), *chaural* (rice), *sabzi* (vegetables), and *gosht* (meat). The meat may be anything except pork, because Muslims are not allowed to eat pork. Spices are often added to meals to flavor them.

Marriage

Most marriages in Pakistan are arranged by parents. Marriage is seen more as a union between families rather than between individuals. A marriage is sometimes arranged before the couple have even met. It is traditional for the bride's family to present gifts of money or goods, called a dowry, to the groom's family.

Religion

Pakistan is an Islamic state, but its constitution guarantees freedom of religion for its citizens. About 97 percent of Pakistanis are Muslim. All Muslims are required to pray five times a day. Worshippers are called to prayer at a mosque—the Muslim place of worship—by an official called a *muezzin*. Women may attend prayers, but it is not a requirement for them.

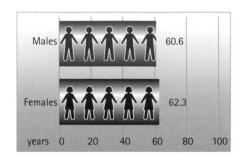

Males		60.6
Females		62.3
years	0 20 40 60 80 100	

Life expectancy in Pakistan is about 15 years less than in many Western countries.

Dress

The national dress of Pakistan is the *shalwar-kameez*. The shalwar is a pair of loose-fitting, ankle-length trousers gathered at the waist. The kameez is a long, shirt-like top. On formal occasions, especially in the cities, women wear saris.

Web Search ►►

► http://www.tourism.gov.pk/religions.html
Facts and figures about religion in Pakistan from the government of Pakistan Web site.

Arts and Media

Cinema, broadcasting, music and magazines all play an important part in Pakistan society. The history of the region and the work of its artists are displayed in Pakistan's many museums and art galleries.

Cinema is the most popular form of entertainment. Small cinemas outside the major cities show mainly locally-made films. Urban cinemas show a mixture of Hollywood action movies and foreign films as well as traditional films. Lahore is the centre of Pakistan's movie industry, which is also known as Lollywood.

Television and newspapers

Pakistan has its own, mainly state-run, television channels, but increasing numbers of people can now receive satellite television. Poorer rural families rely more on radio to receive news and entertainment. Magazines are very popular and offer wide-ranging coverage of current affairs, politics, sport, fashion and entertainment. Foreign newspapers and magazines are available in the cities.

A cinema in Karachi. ▼

Museums and galleries

The National Museum of Pakistan, in Karachi, displays exhibits covering more than 7,000 years of history. Its galleries show pottery, metalwork, textiles and sculptures from different periods. In Karachi, the home of Quaid-e-Azam (Mohammed Ali Jinnah, the founder of Pakistan) has been preserved as a museum. His tomb is nearby and can be visited.

The museum at Moenjo Daro, in Sindh, is on the edge of one of the most important archaeological sites in south Asia. Moenjo Daro is thought to be the world's first planned city. It was built around 4000 BCE. Archaeologists have excavated it and visitors can now walk through it.

An oil painting from the sixteenth century showing men at work on a building site, including sculptors carving elephants. The painting is on display in the Lahore Museum.

Numbers of TV and radio broadcast stations in Pakistan. ▼

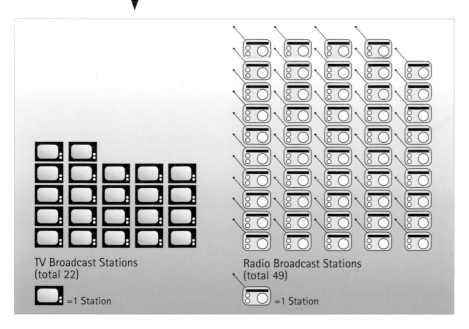

TV Broadcast Stations
(total 22)

▢ =1 Station

Radio Broadcast Stations
(total 49)

◉ =1 Station

Web Search ►►

► http://www.heritage.gov.pk/museums.htm
Details of Pakistan's museums and art galleries, where they are and when they were established.

Government

Pakistan has had a troubled and, at times, violent political past. Its democratically elected governments have been accused of corruption and dismissed by military leaders on several occasions. The latest military coup occurred in 1999, when General Pervez Musharraf seized power.

For administrative purposes, Pakistan is divided into four provinces, one territory, and one capital territory. Each province is made up of between three and eight smaller areas called divisions. These are further divided into more than 100 districts. The disputed region of Kashmir in the northeast includes two districts that are controlled by Pakistan.

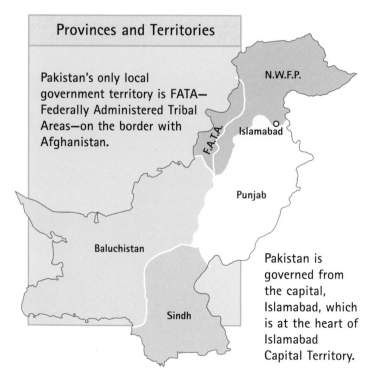

Provinces and Territories

Pakistan's only local government territory is FATA—Federally Administered Tribal Areas—on the border with Afghanistan.

N.W.F.P.

F.A.T.A.

Islamabad

Punjab

Baluchistan

Sindh

Pakistan is governed from the capital, Islamabad, which is at the heart of Islamabad Capital Territory.

The City Hall in Karachi, the capital of Sindh province. ▶▶

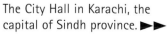

The president and Security Council

The president is the head of the government. The parliament is composed of two houses—the National Assembly and the Senate. The National Assembly has 217 seats. Of these, 207 seats are reserved for Muslim candidates and 10 for non-Muslims, all elected by popular vote. Most of the 87 senators are selected by the provincial assemblies. The remainder, in the tribal areas, are elected by the people. National Assembly members serve for five years, and senators serve for six years. One-third of senators give up their seats every two years. The president is elected for five years by the National Assembly, the Senate, and the four provincial assemblies. The prime minister is elected by the National Assembly.

Parliament was suspended in 1999 after a military coup. The new military president, General Pervez Musharraf, governed with the advice of a National Security Council of military chiefs and cabinet members In 2002, the military leadership began to transfer power back to a newly elected parliament.

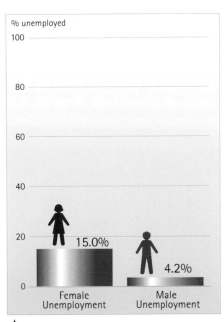

▲▲ Despite political upheavals, unemployment is not especially high, but for religious reasons women often find it hard to get jobs.

◄◄ The royal palace at Hunza, Kashmir, an area in dispute with India over ownership and control. In the background are the Karakoram Mountains.

Web Search ►►

► http://www.tourism.gov.
pk/pakistan_info_.html
*A map showing Pakistan's provinces
and their boundaries.*

Place in the World

DATABASE

Chronology of Historical Events up to CE 1947

c8500 BCE
Settled agriculture begins in Baluchistan

c4000 BCE
The world's first planned city is built at Moenjo Daro

c2600 BCE
Indus Valley civilization begins

1700 BCE
The Indus Valley civilization suddenly disappears

518 BCE
Punjab and Sindh become part of the Persian Empire

195 BCE
Bactrian Greeks invade the region

75 BCE
Scythians capture the Indian subcontinent

53 BCE
Parthians capture northern Pakistan

CE 712
Arab Muslims conquer lower Punjab and Sindh

988
Peshawar comes under Muslim rule

1163
Lahore becomes the capital of the Ghaznavid dynasty

1241
Lahore is sacked by a Mongol army

1524
The Mughals enter Punjab and capture Lahore

1849
Britain takes control of Rawalpindi from its Sikh rulers

1947
British rule in India ends. Pakistan is created

People have lived in south Asia for thousands of years, but the modern Islamic Republic of Pakistan is a young country that is still developing its role in world affairs.

Pakistan is working to improve its economy by increasing exports, reforming its institutions, privatizing many of its industries and rooting out corruption. Pakistan's rapidly growing population places ever-growing demands on its limited resources. The situation has worsened with the arrival of large numbers of refugees from neighbouring Afghanistan. Many of these have fled from the war, led by US forces, to eliminate terrorists responsible for organising the attacks on the USA on 11 September, 2001.

Afghan refugees in Jallozai, a refugee camp in Peshawar, Pakistan. ►►

Pakistan's ongoing dispute with India over the territory of Kashmir has sometimes erupted into violence. As both countries have nuclear weapons, military conflict between them is a matter of international concern. Pakistan's domestic political history has been troubled, too, alternating between civilian government and military rule.

International links

Pakistan participates in many international organizations, including the United Nations (UN) and the World Health Organization (WHO). In addition, it is a member of a number of Asian organizations, including SAARC (the South Asian Association for Regional Co-operation). It is also a member of the Commonwealth, an association of countries that used to be British dependencies. However, following the military coup in 1999 that forced the civilian government to give up control of the country, Pakistan's membership of the Commonwealth was suspended.

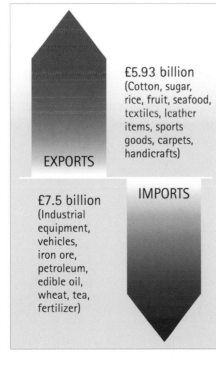

EXPORTS
£5.93 billion
(Cotton, sugar, rice, fruit, seafood, textiles, leather items, sports goods, carpets, handicrafts)

IMPORTS
£7.5 billion
(Industrial equipment, vehicles, iron ore, petroleum, edible oil, wheat, tea, fertilizer)

```
        DATABASE
```

Chronology of Historical Events from 1948

1948
War with India over Kashmir

1958
General Ayub Khan seizes power

1959
Rawalpindi is made the capital city

1965
New war with India over Kashmir

1967
Islamabad becomes the capital city

1969
General Yahya Khan seizes power

1971
East Pakistan becomes Bangladesh. Zulfikar Ali Bhutto becomes Pakistan's prime minister

1977
General Zia ul-Haq seizes power

1979
Zulfikar Ali Bhutto is found guilty of murder and hanged

1988
General Zia dies. Benazir Bhutto is elected prime minister

1998
Pakistani nuclear weapons tests

1999
General Pervez Musharraf seizes power. Pakistan is suspended from the Commonwealth

2002
After new elections, Mir Zafrullah Khan Jamali becomes prime minister under President Musharraf

◄◄ Pakistan's principal exports and imports and their comparative values.

Area:
310,405 square miles
(803,950 sq km)

Population size:
144,616,640

Capital city:
Islamabad (population 201,000)

Other major cities: Karachi
(12,100,000), Lahore (6,350,000),
Faisalabad (1,920,000), Rawalpindi
(920,000), Hyderabad (795,000)

Longest rivers:
Indus (1,800 miles (2,896 km) in
Pakistan), Sutlej (964 miles (1,551
km)), Chenab (772 miles (1,242
km)), Ravi (560 miles (901 km)),
Jhelum (513 miles (825 km)), Beas
(247 miles (398 km))

Highest mountain:
K2, also known as Mount Godwin
Austen (28,251 feet (8,611 m))

Longest glaciers:
Siachin (47 miles (75 km)), Baltoro
(39 miles (62 km)), Batura (34
miles (55 km))

Currency:
Pakistani rupee

Flag:
Green with a vertical white band on
the flagpole side and a white
crescent and star in the middle of
the green part.

Languages:
Official language: Urdu.
English and Punjabi are widely
spoken. Sindhi, Siraiki, Pashtu,
Baluchi, Hindko, Brahui, and
Burushaski are also spoken.

Major resources:
Natural gas, oil, coal, iron ore,
copper, salt, limestone

Major exports:
Textile products, rice, cotton,
leather goods, athletic shoes

**National holidays and major
events:**
March 23: Pakistan Day
May 1: International Labor Day
August 14: Independence Day
September 6: Defense of
    Pakistan Day
September 11: Anniversary of the
    death of Quaid-e-Azam
    (Mohammed Ali Jinnah)
Religious holidays are based on
the lunar calendar and so fall on
different dates each year.

Religions:
Predominantly Muslim, also Hindu
and Christian

30

Glossary

AGRICULTURE
Farming the land, including plowing, planting, raising crops, and raising animals.

ALTITUDE
The height above sea level of a mountain or an area of land.

CASH CROP
A crop grown for sale, especially to another country.

CLIMATE
The long-term weather in an area.

CULTURE
The beliefs, ideas, knowledge, and customs of a group of people, or the group of people themselves.

ECONOMY
The organization of a country's finances.

EMPIRE
A group of colonies—countries in other parts of the world—ruled by one country.

EXPORTS
Products, resources, or goods sold to other countries.

FERTILE
Soil rich in nutrients that make it ideal for growing crops.

GOVERNMENT
A group of people who manage a country, deciding on laws, raising taxes, and organizing health, education, and other national systems and services.

GROSS DOMESTIC PRODUCT
The value of all goods and services produced by a nation in a year.

IMPORTS
Products, resources, or goods brought into the country.

ISLAM
The religious faith of the world's Muslims. Islam was founded by the prophet Muhammad.

LITERACY
The ability to read and write.

LITERACY RATE
The percentage of the population who can read and write.

MANUFACTURING
Making large numbers of the same things by hand or, more commonly, by machine.

MONSOON
A seasonal wind that blows across south Asia from the southwest in summer, bringing heavy rain.

POPULATION
All the people who live in a city, country, region, or other area.

PROVINCE
A part of a country that has a particular identity, often with its own local government.

REPUBLIC
An independent country whose head of state is an elected president, not a king or queen.

RESOURCES
Materials that can be used to make goods or electricity, or to generate income for a country or region.

RURAL
Having the qualities of the countryside, with a low population density.

SUBCONTINENT
A large distinctive land mass that is part of a continent. The Indian land mass, which includes Pakistan, is a subcontinent of Asia.

URBAN
Having the qualities of a city, with a high population density.

Index